IN YOUR SERVICE:
THE VETERAN'S FRIEND

by Galen Maddy

BRANN
PUBLISHING

Tampa, FL

BRANN PUBLISHING
Published by Oculus Media Group
Oculus Media Group, LLC (USA)
Tampa, FL 33543

Produced by Brann Publishing,
a division of Oculus Media LLC, for
The Galen Maddy Group
2897 Brentwood Court
Carlsbad, CA 92008
1-800-451-7019
gmaddy@adelphia.net

Photos are used with permission of the United States Government Archives
Cover Design by Bo Savino

Cataloging-in-Publication Data

Maddy, Galen.
      In your service: the veteran's friend / Galen Maddy.
      Photos: United States Government Archives.
      p. 120.
      ISBN-13: 978-1-934677-25-4; ISBN-10: 1-934677-25-6

LOC# PENDING

PRINTED IN THE UNITED STATES OF AMERICA

10 9 8 7 6 5 4 3 2 1

"The Improved Pension Program (IPP) is a benefit
mandated by Congress for qualifying Veterans
and Surviving Spouses of a period of a war era,
because of non-service connected disability or age."
—*The Veterans Administration*

HERE'S WHAT YOU KNOW:

You're a veteran, or a surviving spouse, either currently residing in an assisted living facility or requiring assistance. You face unreimbursed medical costs that could deplete or eliminate your assets within a few years.

HERE'S WHAT YOU ALSO KNOW:

You or your spouse served this country with distinction during a period of wartime.

HERE'S WHAT YOU MAY NOT KNOW:

You might be missing out on a small fortune in Department of Veterans Affairs benefits—benefits to which your service in wartime entitles you. These benefits guarantee you the dignity of living with quality medical care and financial safety for the rest of your life.

HERE'S WHERE YOU STAND:

You are one of up to 2 million veterans or surviving spouses who may be qualified to receive the Aid & Attendance benefit.

INTERESTED IN KNOWING MORE?

Read this book. As you do so, call the Veteran's Friend Group at 1-800-451-7019. We're here to help you obtain the Veterans Non-Service Connected Disability Pension for you, at no charge.

TABLE OF CONTENTS

"This is a Win-Win-Win-Win situation:

A WIN for the veteran

A WIN for the veteran's family

A WIN for the assisted living facility

A WIN for the representative who helps the veteran
obtain the benefit

There are no losers in this scenario. Forgotten income
is being delivered to forgotten people."

— Galen Jones

*"He served the country.
Now the country is serving his life."*

FOREWORD

by Merwyn S. Miller, J.D.
Attorney at Law

I've known Galen Maddy for almost 30 years. Through his various successful careers as a columnist, author, land banker, mortgage banker and financial advisor, I've found him to be honest, creative and insightful. As a Board Certified Specialist in Estate Planning, Trust and Probate Law*, I've always wanted to work with him.

However, the time was never right.

Then Mr. Maddy, a U.S.M.C. veteran, came to me with an idea: Why not get together and assist veterans, pro bono? "There is this V.A. pension that is available," he told me, "and virtually no one knows about it, and few veterans who are eligible apply."

One thought came to me: Look at all the people we can help at no cost to them!

Suddenly, the time was right. My son had just joined the military to become an Army officer. He had conducted some family research and found out information about my Dad that even I didn't know: Dad had earned three Bronze Stars. That made me very proud and very interested in helping those who had fought for our country.

As I studied the subject, I realized that this pension—the Aid & Attendance Benefit— was for people who served our country

1

during a time of war. If they weren't able to accumulate enough resources to support themselves adequately after they reached old age or became disabled, the country they served would now serve them in their time of need. The assistance would supplement their income. In other words, this program would help veterans, their surviving spouses and families be able to afford a level of dignity that they might not otherwise be able to afford for themselves.

We all know that assisted living facilities, nursing homes and home health care can cost a lot of money—sometimes, an exorbitant amount. It becomes a burden upon the children. Very few seniors desire to burden their children. This pension allows them to avoid putting their children in that position.

Yes, there are income and net worth limits, but with the assistance of an experienced and skilled advisor such as Mr. Maddy, these requirements can be met and the pension obtained. I am proud to be working with Mr. Maddy and to assist his clients in applying for this pension.

That's what both the book and the group, The Veteran's Friend, are about: retaining your dignity!

*Certified by the Board of Legal Specialization, State Bar of California

INTRODUCTION:

The Saga of Uncle Frank

I would like to share a personal experience that I had with a family member, one that led to what I now feel to be an integral part of my latter life's work—serving the men and women who served this country in wartime. My father's youngest brother, Uncle Frank, was a World War II veteran, though he never served overseas during the war. In his later years, after leading a solid, modest life, Uncle Frank checked into an assisted living facility in Duluth, Minn. The family discovered that he would qualify for a Veterans Administration benefit, called the Aid & Attendance Benefit—also known by a typically lengthy bureaucratic name, the Veterans Non-Service Connected Disability Pension.

Now in his late 70s, Uncle Frank had repeatedly corresponded with the V.A. in an attempt to obtain the Aid & Attendance Benefit to help him with the cost of the assisted living community. After he encountered many dead ends and received questionable advice, Uncle Frank grew extremely frustrated with the whole process.

Eventually, Uncle Frank called me. He knew of my career as a financial and estate planner, and of the many years I'd spent navigating the often complicated world of finances, taxes, asset protection and the like. He also knew of my service background in the U.S. Marine Corps. The question he asked both surprised and humbled me: Could I help him apply for the benefit? He was fearful of running out of money before he passed away.

I found it hard to imagine. Here was a man who served his country during our nation's most dire hour—World War II, when we were being threatened by the Third Reich at one end at Japan at the other—and yet, he found it impossible to deal with the V.A. over a benefit to which he was entitled by virtue of serving in wartime!

That was one thing. Quite frankly, I was astounded at the maze of paperwork that was required to fill out for this elder veteran to receive the benefit. After a lengthy period of time, we finally got Uncle Frank approved.

Uncle Frank had roughly $180,000 in his savings, while his total monthly retirement income added up to $1,800 per month. Uncle Frank's expenses, however, were a different story: He faced $4,000 per month in bills. That created a monthly spending deficit of $2,200—better than $26,000 per year. When I did the math, I didn't like what I saw: Without some modification upward in income and/or downward in expenses, Uncle Frank would run out of money in six to seven years.

After we qualified Uncle Frank for the Aid & Attendance Benefit, he received an additional monthly payment of $1,500 from the V.A. This meant that his annual deficit shrank from $26,000 per year to approximately $8,000 per year. Once the first seven years passed—seven years that, originally, looked like they would spell the end of his savings—we estimated that Uncle Frank would have $122,000 or more remaining. If Uncle Frank survived past those seven years, it would enable him to continue living with dignity in the assisted living community.

Living with dignity. That's what we're talking about here. Both Uncle Frank and I wanted him to live without financial worry while continuing to receive the assistance and care required by his medical condition. In my mind, that was the least I could do for him, and the least the government could do for one of its wartime servicemen.

The experience of helping Uncle Frank moved me very deeply. I made a promise to myself that someday, when I had the available time and wherewithal to perform this vital pro bono work, I would help veterans like my Uncle Frank.

Today, I am able to put that promise into practice. It's time to give the estimated 2 million aging or disabled wartime veterans the benefit they richly earned through their service.

Now, I am in your service.

~ Galen Maddy

IN YOUR SERVICE:
THE VETERAN'S FRIEND

by Galen Maddy

CHAPTER 1:

It Doesn't Have to Be This Way

The plight of Uncle Frank and many thousands of others may fill us with compassion, sadness and even horror. After all, didn't he serve with distinction and honor? Didn't he stand in harm's way to protect our country and its ideals? Didn't he give prime years of his life because he believed in a free, democratic society enough to fight for it? Whatever happened to Abraham Lincoln's admonition, "to care for him who shall have borne the battle, and for his widow and orphan…?"

Fortunately, Uncle Frank's situation came to a satisfying conclusion: we were able to qualify him for the Veterans Non-Service Connected Disability Pension—better known by one of its aspects, the Aid & Attendance Benefit. The opposite result is all too common in the United States today. When wartime veterans become disabled or die, many of them or their surviving spouses are left with financial difficulties that range from difficulty to bankruptcy to devastation. Others who thought they'd planned accordingly learn that the cost of long-term medical care, in-home nursing, assisted living facilities or residential care quickly eats up their life savings, and their social security and other limited pension payments cannot keep up with spiraling costs. It seems like a tremendously unfair conclusion to a life story that included so much honor, dignity, integrity and contribution to society.

That brings us to the primary purpose of this book: It doesn't have to be this way. A little-known, underused Department of Veterans Affairs program, available since 1951, exists that can alleviate or eliminate this worst-case scenario: Aid & Attendance. The benefit can assist with costs for a wide variety of needs—assisted living, enhanced independent living, home health care and nursing homes among them.

However, you likely don't know about Aid & Attendance because the government has rarely promoted it, although various veterans organizations from all branches of the armed forces have been distributing information. You can find it on the V.A. website under "Compensation and Pension Benefits," but it takes sharp eyes and a good idea of what you're looking for. Another representative who does tireless work on behalf of wartime veterans, Galen Jones, calls it "forgotten income for forgotten people."

Confused? Don't feel alone. Of the estimated 2 million-plus veterans or surviving spouses that could be eligible for the benefit, only 14% of surviving spouses and 27% of veterans have ever received money. In early 2007, Brad Mayes of Veterans Affairs told *NBC Nightly News*, "We know that about 36 percent of veterans either didn't know about the program or thought they weren't entitled."

Based on the number of veterans to whom I have spoken, I feel Mr. Mayes' estimate is optimistic. I believe that more than half of all veterans don't know about this program—nor would they imagine themselves to be eligible for it if they did know. After all, who gets 20 or 30 years of benefits for serving as few as 90 days, only one of which has to fall during a period of war?

Once in a great while, though, something comes along that

might look too good to be true—*only to actually be true.* Aid &
Attendance is one such benefit.

The number of eligible veterans and surviving spouses is about
to skyrocket, as baby boomer veterans get ready to turn 65 starting in
2011. Seniors in our country are living longer, but their savings are
deteriorating faster than ever by the higher cost of living, healthcare,
and the unfortunate recent problems that befell many pension and
401(k) plans. In 2003, as the war in Iraq ignited, the V.A. began
to clamp down harder on health care enrollments for veterans who
did not have service-connected disabilities (Note: The subject of
this book happens to be about a *non*-service connected disability
pension). In 2003, the V.A. also created what is called "Priority 8,"
barring access to V.A. clinics, hospitals, physicians and medications
for people over certain income limits.

Consequently, according to federal statistics, the V.A. turned
back 17,378 new enrollees in 2004.

Then there are the veterans of the wars in Iraq and Afghanistan,
who currently range in age from 19 or 20 to commanders in their
early- to mid-50s. Many thousands are returning home with no
apparent physical injuries. However, close calls with roadside
bombs and other explosive devices—the killing method of choice
among the insurgents—are leaving many with post-traumatic stress
disorder (PTSD) and undiagnosed traumatic brain injury. Carl
Anderson believes that many returning Iraq and Afghanistan vets
will be forced to file for the Aid & Attendance Benefit in coming
years because their disabilities will not be recognized by the V.A.
as directly war-related. Anderson is a retired clinical professional
and former Marine 1st Lieutenant who worked with World War
II, Korea, Vietnam and Gulf War veterans diagnosed with PTSD
at the 112-bed Veterans Village in San Diego, Calif. (formerly the
Vietnam Veterans of San Diego).

"These veterans will need benefits and assistance as well,"
Anderson said. "I might think their (disabilities) are service-

connected, but the V.A. won't. They might try to tie a behavioral disorder caused by a delayed reaction to an explosive device to the person's dysfunctional childhood. You never know what the V.A.'s reasoning is when denying a compensation or pension program, but I applaud the person, or people, who are filling a helluva void by helping these guys get the Aid & Attendance benefit."

The situation is not going to improve in our present climate of rising healthcare, lodging and living costs, tougher access to insurance and benefits, decreasing numbers of long-term pension or account plans (unless self-created, such as IRAs) and tightening credit. I feel a sense of urgency to inform every potentially eligible wartime veteran about Aid & Attendance and how to obtain it—and to help veterans

who have previously applied for the benefit to re-file in accordance with V.A. regulations, and/or present the proper documentation.

Basic Eligibility

Veterans who served during a period of wartime, or their surviving spouses, are eligible for the Aid & Attendance benefit, *in addition to their regular social security and/or employment pension*, if they meet a specific set of criteria:

1) Must have received other than a dishonorable discharge;

2) Must have served at least 90 days active duty, including one day during a period of war—and the veteran does not have to serve within a battle theater during that minimum one day;

3) Must be at least 65 years of age and/or disabled;

4) Satisfy a formula that includes income and net worth (excluding your house and car), minus medical expenses.

The "Aid & Attendance" moniker has confused countless people, who often associate it with regular military pensions. Let us take a moment to introduce you to its criteria and hopefully clear up any misconceptions or confusion. A disabled veteran or his surviving spouse is eligible if one or more of these definitions of disability apply, regardless of age:

1) A pensioner or surviving spouse residing in a nursing home, which automatically qualifies one for the Aid & Attendance benefit; or

2) Lives in a state of blindness or near-blindness, or suffers from a physical or mental disability that requires the regular Aid & Attendance of another person, either in assisted living or home health aides.

We delve into all the requirements and nuances of this benefit in Chapter 2.

How much monthly aid are we talking about with the Aid & Attendance Benefit? Depending upon a number of income and asset factors (see Chapters 3 and 5), you could receive up to an additional $1,801 per month. Given the spiraling costs of long-term and full-time health care, the extra money can pay home costs, protect assets and savings, and offset other medical costs. In other words, this benefit can protect the retirement—or a surviving spouse's assets—for which you and your family have carefully planned for so many years. Very few actions in our later years are more important to take than protecting and shielding our assets.

In addition, qualification for Aid & Attendance *automatically entitles the veteran to full V.A. health care and prescription benefits as well!*

Many thousands of wartime veterans or their surviving spouses qualify for this benefit. It might be you. It's almost certainly somebody you know—a man with whom you served, a lifelong friend, perhaps a business colleague, maybe someone you met at one of the Veterans' functions you attended over the years.

Sometimes, the benefit arrives at the most crucial time and positively impacts entire families otherwise forced to chip in. Take the case of a World War II veteran from Mead, Kan. He'd previously applied for the benefit, but was denied because the Department of Veteran Affairs service officer failed to show him how to properly transfer $70,000 in assets to meet the qualifications. His three adult children faced a terrible decision as his assets dwindled: either remove him from the assisted living facility in which he lived, or pay for his care from their own pockets. No proud veteran wants his or her kids to pick up the tab.

With the help of veteran's benefactor Galen Jones, the man transferred his assets to his family and reapplied for the benefit. He was approved in three months—close to a speed record, as those of you who have dealt with the V.A. or any other governmental bureaucracy probably know. His first check covered four months

of retroactive monthly payments, which was a good thing, because the man's family had just placed him in the hospital for treatment and were trying to figure out where the extra money for the bill would come from. "We're so appreciative," his daughter wrote. "The checks couldn't have come in a more timely fashion."

Why So Few Have Aid & Attendance

Still, so few take advantage of Aid & Attendance. Why? By now, nearly all of us have dealt with government paperwork in one form or another—whether 1040's with a litany of separate forms that call into play the ponderous IRS tax code; or filings for military medical benefits; or one of countless other dealings with the federal bureaucracy. How about trying to determine the military benefits for which you, a family member or someone you know may qualify? There is the V.A. Disability Compensation, the Special Monthly Compensation for Serious Disabilities, the Dependency and Indemnity Compensation, the V.A. Pension, the Death Pension, the Burial and Memorial Benefits (separate filings for service and nonservice-related deaths), and the benefit this book addresses, the Aid & Attendance Benefit.

Enough to make your head spin, isn't it?

While trying to fill out these forms, many of us have wrung our hands in frustration and even questioned our intelligence. What do they mean? How do we fill these out? How do we determine the proper documentation to send along? What do they want? As veterans and people who've built lives on completing missions and tasks, and finishing what we start, we're doggedly determined to complete the paperwork, turn it in and await the result.

Invariably, something comes back to us either incomplete or improperly filled out. Many thousands have actually filed previously for the Aid & Attendance Benefit, only to be denied by the Department of Veterans Affairs for any number of reasons. Sometimes, we've been denied because we received improper advice from a well-meaning financial advisor or attorney who didn't know the ropes, or because we failed to receive the one piece of information from a V.A. service officer that would have pushed the application through.

To say this can be disorienting and disheartening is an understatement; more accurately, it leaves us disillusioned. We might question why our government can't make our final years easier for us with the simple gesture of providing benefits without blizzards of confusing paperwork and regulations.

The confusion also exists within Department of Veterans Affairs regional offices, which processes the veteran's disability benefits—not the place where you want indecision, lack of knowledge or misunderstanding. In 2004, according to a V.A. "Mystery Caller" program buried deep on the administration's website (out of reach to all but the most savvy web surfers), V.A. claims experts made a total of 1,089 "mystery calls" to regional offices. The callers posed as relatives or friends of Veterans inquiring about possible benefits, including one of its most obscure, Aid & Attendance. The memo concluded:

• 22 percent of the answers callers received were "completely incorrect";
• 23 percent of the answers were "minimally correct";
• 20 percent of the answers were "partially correct";
• 35 percent of the answers were "completely" or "mostly" correct.

While a 35% batting average (.350) measures excellence in baseball, or winning 35% of PGA golf tournaments makes you more proficient than Tiger Woods or Jack Nicklaus, it doesn't say much for the winning percentage of any team sport—let alone a benefit that can define the quality of life and level of care you receive for the rest of your life.

Furthermore, an internal V.A. memo found that "willingness to help" and "courtesy/professionalism" among its workers *decreased* between 2002 and 2004. V.A. workers also used "too much jargon," according to many veterans, according to the memo.

That such a low percentage of competency comes from the very organization meant to assist you with obtaining and utilizing these benefits—benefits you earned through your service to country—is alarming, to say the least.

Please don't take this as a sign that the V.A. has hired nothing but unfriendly types to handle veteran's claims. Most V.A. service officers are compassionate, responsible people who seek to assist veterans, but they either don't know how to locate the veterans, or don't know how to educate veterans on how to fill out the paperwork. Certainly, they are short of creative ideas and wherewithal in the one area more crucial to this process than any others—movement or transferring of financial assets to qualify for the pension. After all, on the complex V.A. website, only five sentences of description appear. Those sentences are filled with confusing words that can lead us in every direction but the one for which we're looking, words such as "pension," "disability," "limited income," "a benefit based on financial need." We'll elaborate on these terms later.

As frustrating jobs go, I would imagine that being a V.A. pension caseworker ranks highly. Unfortunately, their frustration often results in lack of proper timeliness and service to you. That's where I can step in to help.

Purpose of This Book

Typically, once a veteran or surviving spouse learns of the Aid & Attendance Benefit—not an easy task, as I've noted—he or she can take one of three courses of action. Each can be lengthy or difficult; it can take nine months or more to process an application, even with qualified and accredited assistance:

1) Deal with the Department of Veterans Affairs directly;

2) Utilize the services of a V.A.-sponsored organization. An example would be the Veterans of Foreign Wars;

3) Work through a licensed attorney who specializes in V.A. benefits and provides these services *pro bono*. Most attorneys are not familiar with the V.A. application process, which can be somewhat like navigating a labyrinth without a map. Thus, while adept in other matters of law and litigation, they're not experienced and qualified to serve you in this particular area.

The Third Solution

The Veteran's Friend Group specializes in providing the third solution—your best option. Like wily mariners, we know how to sail the treacherous waters of Department of Veterans Affairs benefit forms, the governmental regulations, paperwork requirements and conditions. Think of us in the same way you'd consider a good tax preparer—someone who completely advocates your position while understanding how to deal with the organization to which your forms are headed. We combine the three core skills any veteran needs when applying for Aid & Attendance Benefit, or the other benefits mentioned above: financial planning and advice (Galen Maddy), legal advice (Merwyn Miller) and asset/liability accounting (Len Accardi).

The Veteran's Friend Group is highly motivated by the plight of veterans. As a Marine Corps Veteran who's been working on behalf of veterans in the financial services world since 1968, I fully appreciate the right of each individual to be offered the easiest possible course to a retirement without undue financial and medical pressures. Some of that is up to you—your financial choices and how you saved the money you earned. However, some of it can fall out of your hands, especially when unreimbursed medical costs spiral and you're suddenly faced with an assisted living situation.

In addition, the Veteran's Friend Group holds free workshops for veterans and their families, to create deeper public awareness of the Aid & Attendance Benefit and that help is available to file for the benefit through a licensed attorney.

This book lays everything out in the open about the Aid & Attendance Benefit and your entitlement: How to determine eligibility; the planning process; documents you will need to furnish when applying; determining approved and unapproved assets and income; legal issues; dealing with the V.A. during the review process; and examples of how lives have maintained grace, dignity and honor in large part because of this benefit, while alleviating the financial burden placed upon veterans, surviving spouses and families. We share the stories of clients, colleagues and other experts to illustrate the angles and challenges one can face when seeking this benefit. Then we provide a point-by-point breakdown of how we assist you with completing a process whose importance cannot be understated if you're eligible.

After all, the financial and physical comfort of your life is more important than anything. Especially when you did your part—serving your country in wartime.

CHAPTER 2:

The Aid & Attendance Benefit

Whenever I inform veterans about the V.A.'s Aid & Attendance Benefit, either at workshops or in private conversations, I often hear the same two questions:

"Why didn't I know about this before?"

"How do I receive it?"

Both questions are not only fair, but it's unfortunate that they need to be asked at all. Senior facilities and family members of seniors often pay $500 to $1,500 just to gain and obtain information about the Veterans Non-Service Connected Improved Pension Benefit that has been available for veterans since November 1, 1951 at no charge!

The benefit—which I will also refer to as Aid & Attendance, throughout this book—was created to benefit wartime veterans and surviving spouses who required in-home care or lived in nursing homes or assisted living facilities. The benefit's creators

worked at a time of high patriotism and military involvement, when the nation was enmeshed in Korea while recovering from two devastating World Wars. While veterans benefits were a small fraction of what they are today, the government was trying to care for those who served all the way back to the Spanish-American and Mexican Border Wars. Among other things, the benefit's creators considered ongoing medical costs for veterans and surviving spouses who experienced the dangerous combination of limited income and the inability to fully care for themselves. They also went beyond the call of duty by focusing on veterans who didn't necessarily suffer a wartime injury or injury while in military service, but who simply required additional assistance in their later years.

The Aid & Attendance Benefit was to provide supplemental income to help combat veterans and surviving spouses pay their expenses, protect their core assets and income, and thus live their final years in the dignity they deserved. What a noble program for the men and women, and their spouses, who fought for the freedom of our country!

Now let's fast-forward a little more than a half century. Today, approximately 143,000 veterans or surviving spouses receive the Aid & Attendance Benefit. The pension participation is declining slightly each year as World War II and Korean War veterans or surviving spouses die and are not replaced by newly-qualified veterans—but get ready for an upsurge as knowledge of the benefit becomes more widespread and we begin to understand the number of delayed-diagnosis traumatic brain injuries suffered by veterans of the wars in Iraq and Afghanistan.

Estimates from various sources state that perhaps 300,000 people have heard of the benefit and comprehend it to any degree at all. An in-house phone survey conducted by the Department of Veterans Affairs revealed that only 35 percent of its own benefits claims specialists possessed working knowledge of the benefit. Says Carl Anderson, "One of the problems I saw when I was working in a clinical situation with veterans is that there are myriad forms and programs, all of this paperwork, and we can't keep track of this. Neither can many of the V.A. case workers, quite frankly."

Conversely, there are an estimated 2 million people who may be eligible for the benefit, and approximately $22 billion available to be appropriated by the V.A. for these deserving recipients.

Only 143,000 current recipients of Aid & Attendance? Of a possible 2 million? With the baby-boomer generation, many thousands of whom fought in Vietnam (and many of those disabled for various reasons and thus already eligible based on health criteria) rapidly approaching age 65?

How has this happened? Why hasn't the V.A. connected combat veterans or their surviving spouses with the additional benefit they earned through their service to country in wartime?

Where Are The Veterans?

The answer will likely surprise you as much as it did me: The V.A. doesn't know how to contact the veterans. They don't know where they are.

"We obviously are here for any veteran or survivor who qualifies," said V.A. pensions official Tom Pamperin. "But so many of these people…we don't know who they are, where they are."

Adds Despina Hatton of a senior law program that seeks to help veterans or their widows receive benefits, "Veterans simply don't know about it."

A number of factors could have caused this, but most commonly, veterans moved any number of times and didn't forward their address change to the V.A. Since the vast majority of servicemen and women didn't serve the minimum 20 years required to receive traditional retirement benefits, graded by rank and years of service, or sustain wartime injuries of such severity that they were entitled to disability pay, they didn't pass along the information.

Another reason why more veterans don't receive the benefit is because their applications were denied. In many cases, the V.A. told them their assets were too high, or not transferred properly. In many others, their paperwork was improperly filled out, or submitted incomplete. For some, the culprit was poor advice received by well-meaning financial representatives or attorneys—or maybe people not so scrupulous at all!

A quick peek into the offices of a fellow veterans' benefactor, Las Vegas-based registered investment advisor Stephen Stone, bears this out. When he decided to come to the aid of fellow veterans (he served in the U.S. Marine Corps during the Vietnam Era), Stephen took on and filed more than 65 applications that had been previously filed. "It is so disheartening," he says. "These are people that have filed applications before, but have either filed incorrectly, or without the right information, or have fallen through the cracks because no one was there to help them see it through. We have one lady who re-filed in October 2006, and we still haven't gotten her cleared (as of September 2007) because of issues from a past filing."

Stephen then shared a real heartbreaker: the case of a veteran who was taken in by a Nevada assisted living facility on the premise that his Aid & Attendance application would be approved. When no answer came from the V.A. after 60 days, the assisted living facility had no choice but to evict the man. As of this writing, Stephen is pushing hard to secure the benefit so the veteran can get the care he needs.

Unfortunately, there are many stories like this—which is why folks like Stephen, Galen Jones and Tom Pizer pour over 100 combined years of professional experience into this work. "We're bending over backwards to help these guys," Stephen says.

That's what it takes.

Why Securing Aid & Attendance Is *Not* Big Business

In entrepreneurial, enterprising America, one would expect countless attorneys, accountants and financial planners and advisors to locate these veterans once they learned about Aid & Attendance. After all, we're talking about a monthly benefit that could help fund someone for 20, 30 or even 40 years—perhaps $500,000 for a single long-living beneficiary. Moreover, the work is far more meaningful than something like ambulance chasing: those who enter it are providing the crucial service of helping military veterans who *defended the very freedoms in which these attorneys, accountants and financial advisors and planners have thrived* to apply and navigate the governmental maze toward approval.

Here's the problem: V.A. law prohibits anyone assisting a veteran applying for this particular benefit from being reimbursed for work specifically linked to the application process. An accredited practitioner either works *pro bono*, or not at all. That makes the number of well-qualified and accredited specialists very, very few, which can be very disappointing and disheartening, for the reason I'm about to explain.

When veterans are contacted, or when veterans learn about the Aid & Attendance Benefit and contact the V.A., they learn the benefit is very obscure and information is scarce. As mentioned, only 35 percent of surveyed field office claims specialists possess working knowledge of it. They also learn that the process of obtaining the benefit involves a mountain of paperwork and documentation that is difficult, ponderous and, for many, downright paralyzing. Since veterans or surviving spouses may receive the benefit for 30 or 40 years, the V.A. wants to be sure no fraudulent claims are presented and awarded. In a word, that means paperwork. At a workshop I gave in May 2007, I told attendees that submitting a highly detailed IRS 1040 long form was a piece of cake compared to submitting the documentation for this program.

I'm not kidding. It's tough stuff. Which is why I've put all of my four decades of wherewithal into serving as a *pro bono* advocate for wartime veterans or surviving spouses who wish to qualify for and receive the Aid & Attendance Benefit.

WHAT AID & ATTENDANCE COVERS

The Aid & Attendance Benefit covers the following expenses:

- ✔ Mobility
- ✔ Housekeeping
- ✔ Dressing
- ✔ Grooming
- ✔ Bathing
- ✔ Assistance with use of toilet
- ✔ Meal Preparation
- ✔ Errands
- ✔ Communication
- ✔ Social Interaction
- ✔ Exercises and Therapies for Mental Acuity
- ✔ Chores
- ✔ Other assistances for disability living

Aid & Attendance: The Breakdown

The first step in this process, as in any endeavor, is to gain knowledge of the benefit. What exactly is the Aid & Attendance Benefit? How does it differ from other benefits veterans, retirees, their spouses and family receive from the V.A. and the U.S. government? How does it differ from pensions? Disability income? Social Security?

Let's break it down. The Aid & Attendance Benefit is a pension benefit that may be available to wartime veterans (65 years of age and older, and/or disabled) and surviving spouses who have in-home care or who live in nursing homes or assisted living facilities. The benefit is awarded based on the applicant's net assets and income, and the amount, extent and source of their unreimbursed medical expenses (See: "What Aid & Attendance Covers," page 27).

However, and I want to emphasize the importance of this point:

Many elderly veterans and surviving spouses whose incomes are above the congressionally mandated legal limit for a V.A. pension may still be eligible for a monthly Aid & Attendance check if they have large medical expenses—including nursing home expenses—for which they do not receive reimbursement.

Veterans who served during a period of combat are eligible for this benefit, in addition to their regular pension, if they meet a specific set of criteria:

1) The veteran must have received other than a dishonorable discharge (such as an honorable discharge, retirement, etc.);

2) The veteran must have served at least 90 consecutive days of active military service;

3) That service must include one day during wartime. The veteran is not required to have served within a battle theater during that day, but to have been active duty;

4) The veteran must be at least 65 years of age and/or disabled; and

5) The veteran must satisfy a financial obligation formula that includes income and net worth (excluding your house and car), minus medical expenses.

One of the many wonderful features of Aid & Attendance is that it does not require injury sustained on the battlefield, nor injury sustained during military service at all. Aid & Attendance focuses on medical situations that arise during the course of a veteran's long life. Obviously, if you did receive a Purple Heart or suffered an injury during military service, you're also included as a possible recipient of this benefit.

The second phase concerns medical requirement: To receive the Aid & Attendance Benefit, a recipient must be in need of regular personal assistance. The following conditions fall under this category:

• Bedridden individuals; and/or
• Inability to dress or undress without assistance; and/or
• Inability to care for one's own bodily needs; and/or
• Assistance needed to adjust special prosthetic or orthopedic devices; and/or
• Debilitating physical or mental injuries or illness that require regular assistance. This includes blindness or near-blindness.

If these initial requirements are met, and you wish to apply for the Aid & Attendance Benefit, the V.A. will determine eligibility by adjusting for unreimbursed medical expenses from the veteran's or surviving spouse's total household income through a formula they call IVAP. If the remaining income after these expenses falls below the annual income threshold for the Aid & Attendance Benefit, the V.A. pays the difference between the claimant's household income and the threshold.

This amount, in 2007, runs to a maximum of $18,234 annually ($1,520/month) for a veteran without dependents, $21,615 annually ($1,801/month) for a veteran with one dependent, and another $1,866 annually ($156/month) for each additional dependent. The annual Aid & Attendance income threshold for a surviving spouse is $11,715 annually ($976/month).

That's the Aid & Attendance Benefit. The easy part is to determine if you or someone you know qualifies—a friend, parent, grandparent, uncle, aunt, brother or sister. We've listed the qualifications. If they meet the eligibility and medical requirements, then the final step prior to submitting an application is to determine income qualification. That step leads to the final part of a claimant's job—assembling the documentation to apply for the benefit and protecting vital assets and income in the process. We cover those subjects in the remainder of this book.

How Aid & Attendance Differs From Other Benefits

Aid & Attendance is one of several programs available to military veterans and their families. A quick look at the other programs that also fly under this banner will enable us to see the differences while also emphasizing how important it is to fully understand the subtleties—or locate someone who can assist you through the process:

• *V.A. Disability Compensation:* This tax-free benefit is paid to a veteran because of injuries or diseases that happened while on active duty, or were worsened by military service. It is also paid to certain veterans disabled from V.A. health care.

• *Special Monthly Compensation for Serious Disabilities:* This is additional compensation paid to a veteran who, as a result of military service, incurred the loss or inability to use specific organs or extremities.

• *Dependency and Indemnity Compensation:* Known as DIC, this benefit is paid to eligible survivors of: a military service member who died on active duty; a veteran whose death resulted from a service-related injury or disease; or a veteran whose death resulted from a non service-related injury or disease, and who was receiving, or entitled to receive, V.A. compensation.

• *V.A. Pension:* This pension is paid to wartime veterans with limited income, and who are permanently or totally disabled or age 65 and older. Aid & Attendance is included beneath the V.A. Pension umbrella, but the particular pension mentioned here contains two subtle but significant differences:

1) The disability must be permanent and total
2) No provision is made for surviving spouses

• *Death Pension:* The death pension is a benefit paid to eligible dependents of deceased wartime veterans.

• *Burial and Memorial Benefits:* These are partial reimbursements of an eligible veteran's burial and funeral costs, generally divided into two payments: burial and funeral expense allowance; and plot interment allowance.

Overcoming the Confusion

When I conduct workshops and talk with veterans and their families about the Aid & Attendance benefit, I spend a great deal of time clearing up the confusion surrounding this issue. Why all the fuzziness about details and misunderstanding?

The first bit of confusion concerns the full bureaucratic name for the benefit: the Veteran's Non-Service Connected Improved Pension Benefit. Enough jargon for you? Me, too. The otherwise twisty title does clearly state that this is an improved pension benefit. Anyone in America who's held gainful employment with one company knows that you only receive a pension from your employer after significant service, usually 20 to 30 years. You work for it, you look forward to it, and when you retire, you receive it. The military is no different from the civilian sector: Veterans with 20 or more years of service receive retirement pensions. What many find hard to believe is that a pension exists for veterans who served as few as 90 consecutive days—who were, in effect, employed by the same employer (the Department of Defense) for as little as three months.

Next, one of the Aid & Attendance qualifications is that you must be disabled or over age 65. We would expect a benefit for someone who is disabled as a result of his or her employment, but a benefit that is not employment related? Also, who receives a benefit just for turning 65—unless it is Social Security? Again, examine the name of the benefit—non-service connected. Indeed, there is a benefit available to veterans and their surviving spouses just for being disabled, and just for turning 65—and rightly so.

Finally, there are income and asset limitations connected to this benefit. We all know what the definitions of income and assets are, but have you ever seen the Department of Veterans Affairs' definition? They call it IVAP—Income for Veterans Affairs Purposes. The V.A. arrives at an IVAP calculation by subtracting the UME—un-reimbursed medical expenses—from the initial income. Many do not expect to receive a benefit based in part upon their un-reimbursed medical expenses, but that is exactly what Aid & Attendance addresses.

Unfortunately, all of this alphabet soup can be so confusing that people stop beforehand. Or, worse, file incomplete or incorrect applications that are denied, causing them to stop trying for a benefit that has had their name written on it since their wartime service.

Aid & Attendance rewards the service and sacrifice our veterans and their widows made, and continued to make, throughout the recent history of our country. This improved pension benefit was designed to play—and pay for—a significant role in their lives. It's time to take advantage of this and insure greater comfort and dignity during what should be your most easygoing, peaceful years.

CHAPTER 3:

Who Is Eligible?

The eligibility criteria for the Aid & Attendance benefit is surprisingly simple, and much broader in its reach than one might expect. Because of that, it is estimated that up to 2 million veterans or surviving spouses may be eligible—but only 143,000 are currently receiving the benefit, according to 2007 V.A. figures.

Yet, we're on the cusp of monumental growth in this area. After shrinking by 5,000 to 7,000 people annually for the past several years (owing to deaths of World War II and Korean vets and/or their surviving spouses), that 143,000 figure will likely increase as baby boomers reach their 65th birthdays beginning in 2011. It will also increase as, unfortunately, Vietnam and Gulf War veterans continue to develop permanently disabling health issues that are non-service connected. It's vital to know about this benefit so that you can help yourself, your loved one, or perhaps a relative or friend you think may be eligible.

Veteran Eligibility Chart

STATUS			RESULT
Deceased	*At Home*	*Assisted Living*	
Vet	Spouse		Cannot Apply
	Vet & Spouse		Apply only if Vet has significant medical expenses
	Spouse	Vet	Apply; use both incomes and both medical expenses
		Vet & Spouse	Apply; use both incomes and both medical expenses
Vet		Spouse	Spouse may apply
Spouse	Vet		Vet may apply

General Eligibility

To reiterate what I've already presented in previous chapters, you are eligible to receive this benefit if:

1. You are at least 65 years of age and/or permanently unable to care for yourself;
2. You serve at least 90 consecutive days on active military duty, at least one day of which came during wartime;
3. You are the surviving spouse of a veteran who fulfilled qualification #2, and you are permanently unable to care for yourself;

4. You received other than a dishonorable discharge; and
5. You satisfy a financial obligation formula that includes income and net worth (excluding your house and car), minus unreimbursed medical expenses.

Specific Periods of Wartime

The Aid & Attendance Benefit was created in 1951 to help aging veterans of World War I, the Mexican Border War and the Spanish-American War, as well as disabled servicemen and women from World War II. Now, it covers eligible veterans who served and/or fought during the following wars:

World War II: December 7, 1941 through December 31, 1946

Korean Conflict: June 27, 1950 through January 31, 1955

Vietnam War: August 5, 1964 through May 7, 1975 (Note: Those veterans who served "in-country" prior to August 5, 1964 are considered eligible, dating back to February 28, 1961)

Gulf War: August 2, 1990 through the present (the entire period between the end of hostilities in Spring 1991 and the beginning of the Iraq War in March 2003 are also considered a period of wartime for the purposes of Aid & Attendance and other V.A. disability benefits and pension calculations). An official end date will be set in future by law or Presidential Proclamation.

Additional Factors for Eligibility

1. According to the V.A., anyone who enlisted after September 7, 1980 generally must have served at least 24 months *or* the full period for which called or ordered to active duty.

2. If you or a surviving spouse are at least 65 years of age, and/ or permanently disabled and unable to care for yourself, and you have a live-in dependent who is permanently disabled, that dependent is also eligible to be added to your benefit. If the added dependent is approved, you will receive an additional $156 per month.

In the "Veteran Eligibility Chart," (see page 37) we summarize specific vet-spouse application situations. Please review these carefully.

The surviving spouse is just as deserving of the benefits as his/ her wartime veteran spouse. ***Don't let anyone tell you otherwise.*** It calls to mind a rather incredible story out of Georgia that veterans benefactor Debra Bell told us, a story published in the August 2007 issue of *Senior News* in Atlanta. It involved the 92-year-old widow of Curtis Davis, a Army infantryman who fought in the Battle of the Bulge, then spent 18 months in U.S. military hospitals recovering from his horrific injuries.

In 1997, Mrs. Davis filed for the Aid & Attendance Benefit. She met all of the requirements. Incredibly, a V.A. caseworker told her *that neither she nor her husband deserved it.* What makes this response from the V.A. all the more astonishing is that Mrs. Davis holds in her possession *a Presidential Proclamation thanking Infantryman Davis for his courage* in the Battle of the Bulge.

After being told she didn't deserve the benefit for nearly a decade, Mrs. Davis saw another article and wondered if the benefit was real. When she and her daughter found a benefactor and licensed attorney who could assist her with re-filing, she received the benefit.

This illustrates why it is imperative to find a licensed attorney who is working *pro bono* to help you obtain this benefit, and not to risk your future on tackling the V.A. by yourself.

LIFE EXPECTANCY TABLE

As this chart clearly illustrates, it is very important to apply for and receive the Aid & Attendance Benefit as soon as you qualify. Starting at age 45, we show the life expectancy table as used to determine net worth:

Claimant's Age	Life Expectancy (in years)	Claimant's Age	Life Expectancy (in years)
45	32.1	70	12.6
46	31.3	71	12.0
47	30.4	72	11.5
48	29.5	73	10.9
49	28.7	74	10.4
50	27.8	75	9.9
51	27.0	76	9.3
52	26.1	77	8.9
53	25.3	78	8.4
54	24.5	79	7.9
55	23.7	80	7.5
56	22.9	81	7.0
57	22.2	82	6.6
58	21.4	83	6.2
59	20.6	84	5.9
60	19.9	85	5.6
61	19.2	86	5.3
62	18.5	87	5.0
63	17.8	88	4.7
64	17.1	89	4.4
65	16.4	90	4.1
66	15.7	91	3.8
67	15.1	92	3.5
68	14.4	93	3.2
69	13.8	94-Over	3.0
69	13.2		

Once you determine that you or someone you know is eligible, it's time to move forward and fulfill the proper requirements to claim this benefit. After all, given the ever-growing life expectancy (See "Life Expectancy Table," page 39), you could be looking at hundreds of thousands of dollars in future benefits that will preserve your income and quality of life—every penny of which you've richly deserved through your service.

CHAPTER 4:

At A Planning Meeting

Are you eligible? Ready to receive this well-deserved benefit, or know someone who is? There are three ways to attempt to receive the Aid & Attendance benefit:

1.**Go directly to the V.A.** I don't recommend this approach, because you will be asked to fill out the forms and provide proper documentation mistake-free, and you will receive no assistance. The V.A.'s job is to approve or deny benefits claims, not assist those who make the claims.

2.**Go to an accredited Veterans Service Organization,** such as the Veterans of Foreign Wars (VFW). This can also become quite a challenge, since you will probably need extensive assistance from individuals who are expert in dealing with the V.A. and the mountain of paperwork required to receive Aid & Attendance. If you take this approach, be prepared to do a lot of the work yourself.

3.**Approach a knowledgeable, dedicated, licensed attorney** willing to help you *pro bono*—at no cost for the actual work of preparing, filing and working through the application process. The V.A. requires the attorney helping veterans apply for these benefits to work *pro bono*. It is illegal to charge for this specific service. Besides the Veteran's Friend Group, and myself I know of less than a dozen non-V.A. or veterans service organization-affiliated individuals in the country who are equipped to assist veterans claim the Aid & Attendance Benefit *pro bono*.

Legal Issues

Before proceeding further, I want to further address the legal issues surrounding the *pro bono* work. Like any other service in which billions of dollars are available to be awarded, and millions of potential claimants exist, the business of assisting veterans obtain Aid & Attendance benefits does have its unscrupulous individuals. They aren't many in number, but they do exist. Given the fact you're looking at benefits that will assist you for up to 30 or 40 years, it is vital that you find the right assistance. In Section 5901, Title 38 (U.S.C.), the V.A. clearly states and defines regulations regarding who can and cannot assist you.

Here is what you should look for from myself, my colleagues or any other individual who is making himself available to serve you or someone you know:

1. Is the attorney licensed to practice by a state bar? With the Veteran's Friend Group, Attorney Merwyn Miller is certified by the Board of Legal Specialization, State Bar of California. To be unlicensed or unaccredited is illegal.

2. Is the individual or company suggesting or promoting official government affiliation? If so, this is illegal and should be reported to the V.A..

3. Does the individual or company charge fees to help you with preparing and filing the non-service related improved

pension benefit paperwork? If so, this is a violation of V.A. code. *Pro bono* means free of charge. That's why so few qualified licensed attorneys participate in this type of work. They are too busy with the necessity of conducting and maintaining successful practices.

4. Does the individual or company intend to engage in these types of activities while working on your behalf?
- Gathering information unrelated to the claim;
- Counseling;
- Preparing, presenting or prosecuting claims, like an attorney would if representing you in a court of law or civil court.

If the answer is "yes" to any of these areas, that individual or company is engaging in prohibited activities or unauthorized representation.

As you're seeking assistance, I would also ask the following: What motivates the person? Why is this person putting all of this effort into helping *me*?

The answers from two service providers, Galen Jones and Stephen Stone, shed plenty of light on what you—or I—would want to hear. Says Galen, "I have a friend who had a relative who suffered from Huntington's Disease. My friend did some research and found out about this little-known V.A. benefit. The more I learned about it, the more I realized that I could really help some people who had been all but forgotten by the government."

Adds Stephen, "I'm very proud to have served (in the U.S. Marine Corps). I've been a registered investment advisor since 1966. Now, I'm helping these veterans receive what is theirs to

receive. I'll do anything to help them. The phone can ring 24/7 and I'll be there."

My story amounts to a combination of the others. I found out about the benefit when I helped my Uncle Frank apply and receive it. I've spent the past 40 years doing well in the business of helping others invest, earn, preserve and protect their assets. Many of the clients I've financially advised have been veterans, so I have always kept close tabs with my earlier years, when I served in the U.S. Marine Corps. Now, I'm willing to stick my neck on the line—time and again—to help my fellow wartime veterans obtain the Aid & Attendance Benefit. It's a way to continue serving the country by serving those who put on the uniform.

Planning Your Strategy

Let's say you decide to enlist the *pro bono* services of a licensed attorney, thus making your effort much easier and greatly reducing the number of headaches and level of frustration you would likely encounter otherwise. What happens next?

We schedule an initial consultation—a planning meeting. The atmosphere is relaxed; we can share military stories or discuss our accomplishments and continuing dreams in life, and get to know each other as we work together to secure your Aid & Attendance Benefit. For our first piece of business, we will sign a non-disclosure statement, plus a disclaimer and engagement letter, to put into writing the terms of our working relationship.

Next, we will look at the care you or someone you know is now receiving, the facilities involved, and see if that's the proper place for long-term care in respect to the Aid & Attendance benefit. We will review the eligibility requirements to be sure you meet the service, age and/or disability requirements, then we'll tackle the subject of assets and income, which is critical to determining the final amount of the award (see Chapter 5). We will send you home with a planning worksheet and a checklist of financial and medical documents to gather, then schedule a second meeting to fill out an assets and income worksheet.

A quick review of what we will cover (and what I will furnish you on paper) includes:

1. Collection of Information
    a. General information
    b. Medical expenses
    c. Monthly income
    d. Assets
    e. Additional Information

2. Discuss the two goals of the appointment
    a. Provide more income
    b. Preserve and protect assets

3. Five Actions We Need to Take
    a. See if you qualify for the benefit
    b. Make recommendations for further action
    c. Complete the planning worksheet (together)
    d. Develop an ongoing plan
    e. Develop a spreadsheet of your income and expenses

Required Documents for Planning Meeting

I want you to get the most out of your planning meetings, so that we can move on the application process. Given the slow speed at which the V.A. works (3 to 18 months, depending upon the volume of applications and the preparation of the material; 9 months is the average time from filing to receipt of the first check),

every time shortcut we can create enables you or someone you know to start receiving your Aid & Attendance Benefit faster.

Thus, I strongly recommend you gather available documents required for this process now—whether or not you need the Aid & Attendance Benefit. You just never know when something might happen that changes your status instantly—an accident, debilitating illness, devastating stroke or heart attack. Unfortunately, these are necessary precautions to take as senior citizens. Do your homework while you can. Place these papers with your other vital estate documents, such as your will, durable power of attorney and insurance policies.

A list of required documents for the planning meeting:

1. A copy of a Death Certificate if the veteran is deceased (surviving spouse only)
2. A copy of your Marriage Certificate
3. Copies of all Divorce Decrees
4. A copy of your Driver's License/ID
5. A certified copy of your Military Discharge

6.   A Voided Deposit Slip of your checking account, for V.A. payment
7.   Social Security Statement
8.   A copy of all Banking Statements
9.   A copy of all Investment Statements
10. A copy of all Insurance and Annuity Statements
11. Copies of 401(k)s, 403b, IRAs, 457 plan Statements
12. A copy of your Will
13. A copy of your Revocable Living Trust
14. A copy of Document of Authorizing Person to act on behalf of claimant (if claimant is mentally incompetent)

UNREIMBURSED MEDICAL EXPENSES

The following costs handled out-of-pocket are considered unreimbursed medical expenses for the purpose of obtaining the Aid and Attendance Benefit:

- ☑ Doctor's Fees and Treatments
- ☑ Dental Fees and Treatments
- ☑ Eyeglass Prescriptions and Examinations
- ☑ Medicare Deductions
- ☑ Co-Payments
- ☑ Prescriptions
- ☑ Transportation to and from Medical Facilities
- ☑ Physical, Occupational and/or Cancer Therapies
- ☑ Health Insurance
- ☑ Funeral Expenses
- ☑ Cost of Assisted Living Facilities
- ☑ In-Home Care
- ☑ ADLs

Second Planning Meeting

Once you've gathered your documents, filled out the worksheets and feel you have everything in place to begin the application, we will schedule a second planning meeting with a licensed attorney or his/her paralegal. At that planning meeting, we will go over such things as:

1. Any changes since our last meeting—health, financial, family, etc.
2. Review your current income and expenses.
3. Present the spreadsheet you prepared, and ask the question: Are you better off with or without the Aid & Attendance Benefit?
4. Discuss ways to protect your money.
5. Look at gaining more tax-free income (the Aid & Attendance Benefit).
6. Determine your unreimbursed medical expenses (see "Unreimbursed Medical Expenses," page 48).

After that, we can begin to make your application and start the ball rolling with the V.A.

Steps in Making a Claim

At the planning meetings, the attorney will also familiarize you with the steps necessary to make an Aid & Attendance Benefit claim. I've broken it down to 15 major steps, as follows:

1. Determine the proper care setting and the monthly cost of care.
2. Determine eligibility for pension.
3. Calculate total income, recurring medical expenses, and total assets. In Chapter 5, we address this more directly and include the worksheet we furnish for you to fill out, if you so choose.

4. Decide if the amount of assets will meet an asset test applied by the local regional V.A. office, and make an educated determination as to what that level of assets will be.

5. Apply strategies, if necessary, to reduce the assets.

6. Make an estimate of the pension benefit. If asset transfers are necessary to qualify, the estimate is based on a proposed transfer of assets and readjustment of income.

7. Apply the asset transfer strategies necessary to qualify for this benefit. This might include the establishment of a Qvap Trust, an ingenious asset preservation tool devised by my colleague, Merwyn Miller (see Chapter 6).

8. Obtain the DD 214 or equivalent document.

9. Arrange a physical examination, or arrange completion of the report from the claimant's attending physician to be used for requesting a rating from the V.A.

10. Make sure that the care arrangements are in place and monies have been applied or arranged for the cost before making application.

11. Determine whether power of attorney and/or fiduciary is a requirement with the claim application. If applicable, prepare the proper paperwork for submission.

12. Gather the necessary forms and documents to verify the costs of recurring, unreimbursed medical expenses and to request annualization of those costs.

13. Fill out the appropriate claims forms, and submit it with the applicable documentation listed above.

14. Coordinate additional requests from the regional V.A. office.

15. Attempt to correct any impediments that cause a denial of the claim, and, if possible, submit new evidence to reopen the claim.

The Aid & Attendance Benefit exists for you or someone you know to receive additional tax-free income for your assisted care and unreimbursed medical expenses, preserving your assets, and enhancing your overall income. We turn to that now.

CHAPTER 5:

Protect Your Assets, Secure Your Pension

While planning for your retirement years, and particularly when considering current or future medical issues, three questions should automatically arise when it concerns money:

1) How am I preserving or even increasing my income?
2) How am I preserving my assets?
3) How am I protecting and shielding my assets?

When it comes to qualifying for the Aid & Attendance Benefit, all of these questions take on an even greater importance. I would venture to say this assumes a "life and death" importance for many, because for veterans with limited incomes and modest or little assets, the continued quality and dignity of life is often at stake.

That is why, when the attorney and I meet with veterans to discuss eligibility for the Aid & Attendance benefit and filling out the V.A. paperwork to receive the benefit, I place emphasis on the financial picture. We spend a great deal of time making sure that you understand exactly how and why the current state and position of your income and assets increases or decreases your chances of receiving the benefit—and of cushioning and financing your current or future unreimbursed medical expenses or assisted living needs.

I'm reminded of the example Galen Jones shared of the World War II veteran in Kansas who needed to move $70,000 in assets to his children's name or an irrevocable trust to qualify for the benefit, a simple financial action that any caring representative would have recommended. However, the man initially applied directly through the V.A., whose assigned service officer didn't tell him how to transfer the assets. Nor did he tell the veteran that he *could* transfer them. Thus, the man was denied, but reapplied with Galen's assistance, made the transfer, and received the benefit.

IMPROVED PENSION RATE TABLE

Category	Maximum Annually	Maximum Monthly
Veteran Aid & Attendance Without dependents	$18,234	$1,519
Veteran Aid & Attendance With One Dependent	$21,615	$1,801
One Eligible Veteran Married To Another Eligible Veteran	$14,313	$1,193
Aid & Attendance for Surviving Spouse	$11,715	$ 976

*NOTE: Figures are for 2007. The V.A. provides a slight increase each year, tied to the cost-of-living adjustment.

1. Preserving and Increasing Income

Put simply, the Aid & Attendance Benefit gives the Veteran the golden opportunity to increase income while preserving existing income. The benefit can amount to as much as $1,801 per month for the rest of a married Veteran's life (or $2,346 for two Veterans married to each other), which can make an enormous difference for anyone with a limited, fixed income who needs ongoing medical care and cannot fully care for himself/herself (See "Improved Pension Rate Table", page 54). It is comparable to a Senior saving more than $500,000 in his/her lifetime, putting it into a CD that yields 5% annually and living off the interest—all for serving in the military as little as 90 consecutive days, in which only *one day* had to be during a period of war. Amazing, this benefit…isn't it?

When coupled with the other three elements of our financial protection strategy, this boost in monthly income can offset assisted living and other non-reimbursable medical expenses and preserve existing assets. Our primary purpose in working with you is to tilt the existing equation so that your income increases and the benefit pays the bulk of your non-reimbursable expenses, not your savings and other assets for which you've worked so hard your entire life.

Also, I'd like to point out that we're not talking only about veterans on small, limited fixed incomes. For those with higher incomes, it is easy to assume that you would not qualify for the Aid & Attendance Benefit, because your income is too great. Not many of us would believe that a veteran or surviving spouse earning $3,000 per month would receive a "limited income" designation. What about someone who earns $5,000 per month? Or even $7,000 per month?

According to the income considered by the V.A.—the Income for Veterans Affairs Purposes, or IVAP—even persons earning healthy retirement pay and pensions may be eligible for the benefit. The V.A.'s formula for deriving this net income figure is so complex and confusing that it behooves you to seek the assistance of someone accredited to help you determine if you're rightfully entitled to this benefit. Please don't conclude the V.A. is intentionally creating confusion with calculations such as IVAP to prevent you from receiving Aid & Attendance. The language is broad and complex enough in its scope to allow individual explanations for individual claimants. If you have considerable monthly unreimbursed medical expenses and assisted living costs, and those are subtracted from your monthly income, you'll likely find yourself in the range of eligibility—even if you enjoy a higher retirement income.

Regardless of your monthly income, do yourself the favor of seeing an accredited and qualified individual who can help you work out the IVAP calculation to determine if you are eligible.

FOR UNCLE FRANK'S BENEFIT —AND YOURS

Let's revisit my Uncle Frank, and look at the two scenarios he faced: one with the Aid & Attendance Benefit, and one without. When you review these numbers, think of Uncle Frank as yourself—then look at how beneficial the Aid & Attendance Benefit can be for your short- and long-term future and the dignity and quality of your latter years.

I. If Uncle Frank Did Nothing

INCOME

Social Security	$1,000.00
Pension	$ 800.00
Total Income	$1,800.00

EXPENSES

Assisted Living Facility	$3,800.00
ADL Expenses	$ 200.00
Total Expenses	$4,000.00

Monthly Deficit	($2,200.00)
Annual Deficit	($26,400.00)

II. If Uncle Frank Receives Aid & Attendance

INCOME

Social Security	$1,000.00
Pension	$ 800.00
Aid & Attendance Benefit	$1,519.00
Total Income	$3,319.00

EXPENSES

Assisted Living Facility	$3,800.00
ADL Expenses	$ 200.00
Total Expenses	$4,000.00

Monthly Deficit	($ 681.00)
Annual Deficit	($8,172.00)

STATUS OF UNCLE FRANK'S ANNUAL ASSETS

Year	Without Aid & Attendance	With Aid & Attendance
---	$180,000	$180,000
1	$153,600	$171,828
2	$127,200	$163,656
3	$100,800	$155,484
4	$ 74,400	$147,312
5	$ 48,000	$139,140
6	$ 21,600	$130,968
7	($ 4,800)	**$122,796**
8	($ 31,200)	**$114,624**
9	($ 57,600)	**$106,452**
10	($ 84,000)	**$ 98,280**

(I've **bold-faced** the additional years of comfortable living Uncle Frank stood to enjoy from applying for and receiving the benefit. If you stretch the right-hand column to the point where the assets are exhausted, it goes to 22 years.)

2. Preserving Assets

I introduced *In Your Service* by sharing the story of my Uncle Frank, who asked me for assistance in securing the Aid & Attendance Benefit from the V.A. I explained how the prospect for the rest of his life changed from a seven-year, medically induced loss of his assets to a future that featured solid asset preservation—and with it, the continued dignity of his life in an assisted living facility.

The way we turned the tables for Uncle Frank clearly illustrates the other immediate advantage of receiving the Aid & Attendance Benefit: the Veteran's assets stand a much better chance of being preserved (see "For Uncle Frank's Benefit—And Yours", page 57). Suddenly, Uncle Frank could stop worrying about the erosion of his assets, now that the Aid & Attendance Benefit would combine with his other income sources to pay the V.A.'s majority of his monthly expenses.

It's a case of simple math: If the difference in monthly deficit reduces from a potential $2,200 per month to $681 per month, as it did for Uncle Frank, then assets will be preserved for much, much longer. Please note that in these figures, I do not consider even the most conservative investment strategies, such as CDs, Money Market accounts or T-bills. To emphasize how the Aid & Attendance benefit changes the future of a limited-income Veteran immediately upon its acceptance, I'm presenting this as if the cash was under the mattress, so to speak, to be paid out every month. In Uncle Frank's case, he could dip under the mattress without doing anything else for 22 years—not the seven-year period he was facing when he first asked me for assistance.

Our work isn't necessarily done once you receive the benefit. We have to preserve those assets. That reminds me of Margaret Powell, a Las Vegas-based widow of a World War II veteran. Margaret was already receiving Aid & Attendance, which partially paid for her care. In continuing the process of protecting Margaret's assets, my friend Stephen Stone discovered that her mutual funds were in a high-risk situation given the volatile stock market. She was in no financial standing to take a hit, which would have jeopardized her continued living in an assisted care facility. Stephen re-positioned her assets into a risk-free portfolio, an alert action for which she thanks him every time he talks to her.

Of course, we're not going to allow your assets to sit beneath mattresses. But that illustrates why every eligible wartime veteran or surviving spouse needs to contact a licensed attorney to assist with the *pro bono* filing of application papers and supporting documents for the Aid & Attendance benefit.

Preserving assets is highly important for any senior citizen. For the veteran or surviving spouse on a limited income, it is vital. There is nothing of greater concern for someone looking at years of remaining life, and it is crucial that we secure the Aid & Attendance benefit to give the veteran this assurance.

Asset Evaluation Chart

When we sit down for our planning meeting, I will present you with forms to fill out. They will enable us to review all of your assets and make informed decisions on how to protect and preserve them while qualifying you for the Aid & Attendance Benefit. Some of the items on those forms include:

Social Security Income   Pension Income
Additional Pension Income   Long-term Care Insurance
Trust Deed Income   Interest Income   Dividend Income
Income from Rental Properties and/or Farm

Value of Home
Value of Second and Additional Homes

CDs   Stocks   Bonds
Mutual Funds   Annuities   Bank Checking
Savings Accounts   Cash   Trust Deeds
Cash Value of Life Insurance Policies

IRAs   401(k)s
457 Plans (for retired firefighters)
403(b) Plans (for retired teachers and educational system employees)
TSPs (Thrift Savings Plans)
TSAs (Tax-Sheltered Annuities)

Additional Assets

(**Note:** *Anything you reveal to me in our planning is kept in the strictest confidence by the confidentiality agreements we both sign. The information will be used only to assist the law firm during the* pro bono *work to file the claim application on your behalf.*)

3. Protecting and Shielding Assets

When we sit down to determine your eligibility for the Aid & Attendance Benefit, we work hard to add up your Net Worth—which you may already know. The reasons are two-fold:

a. We need to see if you're currently above the V.A.'s net asset limit for the benefit ($180,000); and

b. If you do exceed it, we need to discuss ways to protect your assets and even shield them while working through the Income for Veterans Affairs Purposes (IVAP) financial formula the V.A. uses to determine your eligibility.

Our goal is to identify your assets (See "Asset Evaluation Chart," page 61). We will need to assess all of your income sources, including those that are not countable toward the figures we present to the V.A. — SSI, TANF, State Temporary Disability Assistance, General Assistance and Home Relief, if you happen to receive any of those. They are all considered welfare-based payments.

We then see how we can utilize the IVAP formula and other financial instruments, including the innovative Qvap Trust (see Chapter 6), to protect and shield the assets for which you've worked your entire life—and pick up the Aid & Attendance Benefit that your service in wartime affords you.

An incredible example of the hidden flexibility in this formula—and the V.A.'s rules—comes from Stephen Stone's files. World War II veteran John Scolario and his wife, Mary, applied for the Aid & Attendance benefit. John suffered from Alzheimer's, and Mary realized the cost of long-term assisted care would eat at their assets, which totaled $350,000—a high number, one would think, for applying for any benefit. Certainly, despite the Scolarios' desire to shield their assets for their children, they were too high to apply for this benefit as well…right?

Here's what happened. Most government pensions and programs, like Social Security and Medicaid, have five-year "look-back" windows, where they review how assets accumulated, were transferred (or not), etc. Incredible, the Department of Veterans Affairs does not. Thus, the Scolarios could reposition their assets to their children, or place them in an irrevocable trust—in either case, out of their direct hands. They did this, and John Scolario picked up the maximum benefit of $1,801 per month. They would not have received the benefit had they gone directly to the V.A., because it would not have been explained to them.

The Scolarios' story doesn't end there. The V.A. allows anyone to give money to a veteran or surviving spouse for maintenance care without counting it as income, provided the money is a steady monthly amount. In other words, you could give John Scolario $3,000 per month, every month, and fall within the rules affixed to receiving the benefit. However, I could not give John $1,000 in October, $1,500 in November and, because I needed to buy Christmas presents, $500 for December. My contribution would be counted as income for John, because it was sporadic. It would violate the V.A.'s restrictions. Your steady payments would not be counted as income.

Let's look into another creative tool for shielding your assets in order to obtain the benefit.

CHAPTER 6:

The Qvap Trust:
Have Your Cake and Eat It, Too!

Often, a Veteran who owns a home wishes to receive the Veterans Non-Service Connected Disability Pension—the Aid & Attendance Benefit. Many times, this Veteran resides in an Assisted Living Facility (ALF). The good news: The home goes down as an uncounted asset for this V.A. program.

However, in many of these cases, the Veteran and his family need the money from the home to help pay for living expenses at the ALF. This means the home needs to be sold, an agonizing decision that can be equally harsh financially when it comes to receiving additional benefits. Typically, if the Veteran is receiving the Aid & Attendance Benefit at the time the home is sold and he receives the proceeds, he will be disqualified from the program.

This problem can be avoided by transferring the house to the children before applying for the Aid & Attendance Benefit—if the children sell the house and use the proceeds to assist the Veteran with expenses. However, the exclusion from capital gains for income tax purposes (up to $250,000 for a single/widowed/

divorced Veteran or $500,000 for a married Veteran) will not be available, and tax will have to be paid. This additional tax could cost the family up to $100,000, assuming a 15% Federal and 5% State income tax.

This places the family in a dilemma: Wait to apply for the benefit while the home is being marketed—a process that can take eight months or more? Or apply for the pension now and pay the extra income tax?

When the claimant has more than one goal—in this case, obtaining the benefit now and avoiding the payment of extra income tax—a Trust of some sort is the answer. However, a normal Living Trust will not work. Assets in a Living Trust remain within the control of the Veteran; therefore, they are viewed by the V.A. as still owned by the Veteran. Assuming the assets are more than allowable (see Chapter 5), the Veteran would be disqualified from receiving the Aid & Attendance Benefit.

Another type of Trust is called for. What about Irrevocable Trusts? They've been used extensively in this field. Case closed, right?

Not necessarily. An Irrevocable Trust places the assets beyond the control of the Veteran and does not interfere with qualification for the pension. That's one of several good reasons why they've been used in lieu of transferring the Veteran's assets to his or her children. Another might pertain to cases in which the Veteran has more than one child, but the desire is for only one to manage the assets—say, another child is a spendthrift who cannot handle money. Still another scenario: The Veteran desires to protect the transferred assets from being passed to his ex-wife in a divorce settlement, or seized by his child's creditors in a lawsuit. Sometimes, the Veteran simply likes the idea of the assets sitting in a Trust rather than the children's pockets while the Veteran is still alive.

But there is a catch: While Irrevocable Trusts do not interfere with qualification for the V.A. pension, typically they cannot avoid the increased income tax problem when the home is sold.

QVAP TRUST GUIDELINES

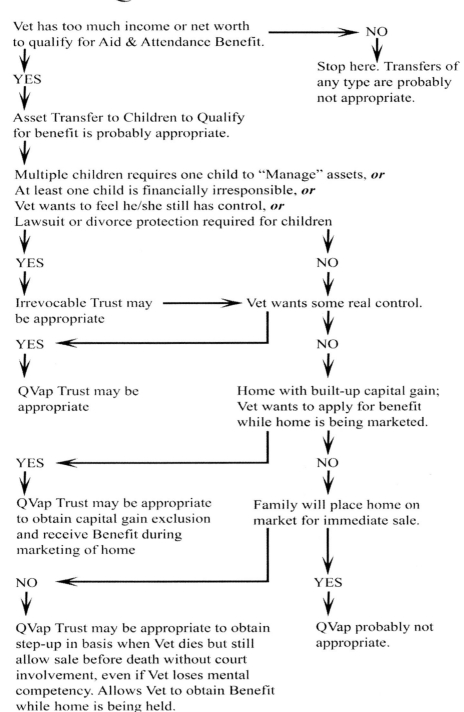

Vet has too much income or net worth to qualify for Aid & Attendance Benefit. → NO

NO → Stop here. Transfers of any type are probably not appropriate.

YES

Asset Transfer to Children to Qualify for benefit is probably appropriate.

Multiple children requires one child to "Manage" assets, *or*
At least one child is financially irresponsible, *or*
Vet wants to feel he/she still has control, *or*
Lawsuit or divorce protection required for children

YES

Irrevocable Trust may be appropriate → Vet wants some real control.

NO

YES

QVap Trust may be appropriate

Home with built-up capital gain; Vet wants to apply for benefit while home is being marketed.

NO

YES

QVap Trust may be appropriate to obtain capital gain exclusion and receive Benefit during marketing of home

Family will place home on market for immediate sale.

NO

YES

QVap Trust may be appropriate to obtain step-up in basis when Vet dies but still allow sale before death without court involvement, even if Vet loses mental competency. Allows Vet to obtain Benefit while home is being held.

QVap probably not appropriate.

We need another type of Trust to solve the income tax problem—a Trust that is a Godsend for Veterans of some financial means who apply for the Aid & Attendance Benefit. Consider the Qvap Trust. Unfortunately, a Veteran can disqualify himself by selling his home to help pay for assisted living, as we've pointed out—or suffer dire tax consequences, if using an Irrevocable Trust. However, he can alleviate that problem with the Qvap Trust. The Qvap Trust offers a way to preserve capital gains treatment on the transfer of homes so that the Veteran does not lose the home or have to spend down the proceeds.

By adding several special clauses, the Trust avoids the increased income tax by allowing the Veteran to claim the exclusion from capital gains while retaining full eligibility for the benefit.

There are numerous benefits to the Qvap Trust (see page 67). If the family is not sure whether or not the house needs to be sold, the Qvap provides a far superior solution to the typical Irrevocable Trust.

Let's take an example that, unfortunately, is fairly common: a Veteran continues to own his/her house while he/she receives the Aid & Attendance Benefit. However, he/she loses mental competence when it's time to sell. That would create a problem. In most cases, there would be no documents in place—or, perhaps, the wrong documents—to legal transfer authority to make the sale and allow that person to sign the title documents. The family would be forced to go to court to obtain a court order allowing the sale. This could add up to many thousands of dollars in legal fees and court costs.

Further, the problem would not be recognized until a buyer was found and escrow began. What if the buyer pulled out of escrow while the court case was proceeding (a process that can last from a few weeks to several months)? Would another eight months of real estate marketing time ensue?

With the Qvap Trust, the house could be sold without the Veteran's signature, so his diminished mental state or mental

incompetence would cause no delays in the sale. If the house never needed to be sold to raise cash for medical treatment, the children could sell the house following the Veteran's death and avoid all income tax on the pre-death capital gain (referred to as the "step up" in income tax basis).

As a bonus, with the Qvap Trust, the Veteran can retain some control on his/her assets and how they're dispersed and used by the children.

That's like having your cake and eating it, too!

(Many thanks to Encinitas, Calif. attorney Merwyn J. Miller for compiling this chapter and developing the Qvap Trust. He can be reached at 760-436-8832)

CHAPTER 7:

Good Endings:
The Benefit in Action

An 83-year-old woman suffering from Alzheimer's learned that the service of her late husband, a Navy medic during World War II, made her eligible for the Aid & Attendance Benefit. She received enough money to help her daughter and son-in-law pay for the assisted living facility in which she lives, guaranteeing residence there, and something she loves—singing.

How about the story of 91-year-old Toivo Nevala, a World War II Army Veteran? According to his family, he never knew he was entitled to V.A. benefits and never filed for any until catastrophe struck. He suffered a massive heart attack, prompting his family to search for a care facility in Nevada for he and his wife, who languished with Alzheimer's Disease. Thanks to accredited elder-law attorney Reiter Feld, the Nevalas applied for Aid & Attendance and received a $1,500 monthly benefit, enabling them to live in the assisted care facility. "Without it, we couldn't make it. Money only goes so far, and they aren't that well off," a niece said.

Stories such as these are the tip of the iceberg when it comes to how the Aid & Attendance benefit has changed, eased and dignified lives. Every time I hear them—or participate in them—my heart warms a little more. I also know there are many, many people who could also be experiencing these positive impacts in their lives, but instead, they're wringing their hands and wondering how in the world they're going to get past the V.A.'s red tape, shield their assets and pay the mounting bills.

My response is to ask you to visit with an attorney who is licensed, or an accredited Veterans Service Organization, to prepare, file and see your application through the process. Sometimes, the action you take to let us serve you can literally come in the nick of time to maintain the assisted living care you, or a loved one, is receiving.

An example of this comes out of Indiana, where one of the most popular men in an assisted living community of 100 residents was on the verge of being evicted. He was out of money, and had nowhere to turn—except to that "forgotten income for forgotten people," the Aid & Attendance Benefit. Galen Jones was trying to set up a seminar on the benefit at the facility. A caring administrator asked him to speak with the Veteran. Galen did, and assured the man he would secure the benefit that would enable him to stay. Galen worked at lightning speed, endured the insufferable waiting period with the man, and delivered. The Veteran received his first check, retroactive for several months, shortly before the facility would have been forced to evict him.

Then there's Rose Davidson, now 74, the widow of a World War II sailor who tried to live on $9,732 per year in Social Security benefits. Frail, legally blind, suffering dementia and in need of regular assistance at home, she was eligible to receive another $1,608 per year in V.A. benefits attributed to her husband's wartime service. That's an additional 17 percent—enough to make a huge difference to one with low income. Not only that, but, as I noted earlier in the book, Aid & Attendance qualification provided her with V.A. health care and prescription benefits as well.

These are just a few examples of Veterans and surviving spouses whose financial burdens were eased by the receipt of the Aid & Attendance Benefit. My Uncle Frank, whose story I shared earlier, was another. Our files contain many other success stories, and others in the process of happening.

As I continue assisting Veterans, surviving spouses and their families, by attending my workshops that introduce and explain Aid & Attendance, I am amazed by the stories I hear. I am equally amazed by the way hope returns to the eyes of Veterans and family members when they realize that, yes, there is a way to alleviate the awful physical and financial burden of elder care when assisted living or disability is involved. Then hope transforms into joy and relief when they realize that, yes, we can work to protect, preserve and shield their existing assets in a host of ways, from reallocating monies to creating Qvap Trusts as designed by my friend and colleague, attorney Merv Miller.

Sometimes, the recipients just can't hold back their relief. An 85-year-old surviving spouse from Leavenworth, Kan. was racking up more than $2,000 per month in costs at an assisted living facility, severely dwindling a nest egg that once stood at $120,000—not a large figure to begin with. She met with Galen Jones, who applied and secured for her the maximum Aid & Attendance benefit for surviving spouses, $976 per month. That plugged the hole in the dam, and preserved the woman's assets and her status at the assisted living facility.

"When I told her that I could get her the benefit, she broke out in tears," Galen recalls. "She could hardly walk, but she stood up, hobbled over to me and kept hugging me.

"This story could be repeated a million times, if we can just get to these people and get them to believe that they're entitled to this benefit."

He's right. All that hope, joy and relief adds up to the real reason why I've reached out to you, and the real reason why you sat down to read this book: to assure yourself, your loved one, your parent or your friend the quality and dignity of life to which every wartime Veteran in this nation should be entitled—without financially breaking the Veteran or, perhaps, those around him or her.

"I can tell you what it's like from inside the clinic," says Carl Anderson, the former Vietnam Marine platoon commander and retired clinical professional at Veterans Village in San Diego. "When one of our patients gets the benefit, we get excited for him. When it happens again, you think, 'Maybe we can really help these guys out.' For some of them, the benefit is literally the difference between life and death—especially when they get discouraged and feel like they can't control their lives anymore.

"We have to get them something. These people need advocates. For a lot of guys, that means going for the non-service connected pension (Aid & Attendance benefit). I don't know of any social worker in the V.A. system who really understands this thing, and

Veterans Service Organizations specialize in helping vets get service-connected disability pensions—Aid & Attendance is not what they're about. Find the people who understand this benefit, and know how to get it. They're filling a helluva void."

Add your story to the successful applications of Aid & Attendance. Find a licensed attorney who will work *pro bono*, then apply for, receive and utilize money that is already set aside for you. It is this nation's "thank you" salute to you for your service.

The widow of Battle of the Bulge veteran Curtis Davis (L) shows his Presidential Proclamation and her first Aid & Attendance Benefit check, secured with the assistance of Debra Bell (R).

APPENDICES

APPENDIX A:

Required Documents for
First Planning Meeting

You will need the following documents for your first planning meeting with The Veteran's Friend Group and the licensed attorney providing this *pro bono* service:

1. A copy of a Death Certificate if the veteran is deceased (surviving spouse only).
2. A copy of your Marriage Certificate.
3. Copies of all Divorce Decrees.
4. A copy of your Drivers License/ID.
5. A certified copy of your Military Discharge.
6. A Voided Deposit Slip of your checking account, for V.A. payment.
7. Social Security Statement.
8. A copy of all Banking Statements.
9. A copy of all Investment Statements.
10. A copy of all Insurance and Annuity Statements.
11. Copies of 401(k)s, 403b, IRAs, 457 and any other pension plan Statements.
12. A copy of your Will.
13. A copy of your Revocable Living Trust.
14. A copy of Document of Authorizing Person to act on behalf of claimant (if claimant is mentally incompetent).

APPENDIX B:
Medical Expenses to Consider

The Veterans Administration lists the following medical expenses in its calculation of Aid & Attendance Benefits:

Abdominal supports
Acupuncture service
Ambulance hire
Anesthesiologist
Arch supports
Artificial limbs and teeth
Back supports
Braces
Cardiographs
Chiropodist
Chiropractor
Convalescent home (medical treatment only)
Crutches
Dental Service (cleaning, X Rays, filling teeth)
Dentures
Dermatologist
Eyeglasses
Food or beverages specially prescribed by a physician
    (for treatment of illness, and in addition to, not as
    a substitute for, regular diet. Physician's statement
    required.)
Gynecologist
Hearing aids and batteries
Home health services
Hospital expenses

Insulin treatment
Insurance premiums (for medical insurance only)
Invalid chair
Lab tests
Lip reading lessons (to overcome a disability)
Neurologist
Nursing services (for medical care, including nurse's
 board paid by claimant)
Occupational therapist
Ophthalmologist
Optician
Optometrist
Oral surgery
Osteopath (licensed)
Physical examinations
Physician
Physical therapy
Podiatrist
Prescriptions and Drugs
Psychiatrist
Psychoanalyst
Psychologist
Psychotherapy
Radium therapy
Sacroiliac belt
Seeing-eye dog and maintenance
Speech therapist
Splints
Supplementary medical insurance (under Medicare)
Surgeon
Telephone/teletype special communications equipment
 for the deaf

Transportation expenses for medical purposes (plus parking, tolls, bus/taxi fares)

Vaccines

Vitamins prescribed by a doctor (but not as food supplement or to preserve general health)

Wheelchairs

Whirlpool baths for medical purposes

X-rays

APPENDIX C:

15 Steps to Making An Aid & Attendance Benefit Claim

1. Determine the proper care setting and the monthly cost of care.
2. Determine eligibility for pension.
3. Calculate total income, recurring medical expenses, and total assets. In Chapter 5, we address this more directly and include the worksheet we furnish for you to fill out, if you so choose.
4. Decide if the amount of assets will meet an asset test applied by the local regional V.A. office, and make an educated determination as to what that level of assets will be.
5. Apply strategies, if necessary, to reduce the assets.
6. Make an estimate of the pension benefit. If asset transfers are necessary to qualify, the estimate is based on a proposed transfer of assets and readjustment of income.
7. Apply the asset transfer strategies necessary to qualify for this benefit. This might include the establishment of a Qvap Trust, an ingenious asset preservation tool devised by one of my colleagues, Merwyn Miller (see Chapter 6).
8. Obtain the DD 214 or equivalent document.
9. Arrange a physical examination, or arrange completion of the report from the claimant's attending physician to be used for requesting a rating from the V.A.

10. Make sure that the care arrangements are in place and monies have been applied or arranged for the cost before making application.
11. Determine whether power of attorney and/or fiduciary are a requirement with the claim application. If applicable, prepare the proper paperwork for submission.
12. Gather the necessary forms and documents to verify the costs of recurring, unreimbursed medical expenses and to request annualization of those costs.
13. Fill out the appropriate claims forms, and submit it with the applicable documentation listed above.
14. Coordinate additional requests from the regional V.A. office.
15. Attempt to correct any impediments that cause a denial of the claim, and, if possible, submit new evidence to reopen the claim.

ORDERING THIS BOOK

Do you have a service group, organization, or a group of friends or fellow veterans who could benefit directly from reading *In Your Service* and taking steps to apply for the Veteran's Non-Service Connected Disability Pension—Aid & Attendance? Are you coordinating or planning to attend a reunion with fellow servicemen or women, or working with veterans to help them learn more about the benefits to which they may be entitled?

If so, then we'd like to give you every opportunity to order *In Your Service*. You can order individual copies from this office, or direct from www.amazon.com or www.brannpublishing.com.

For multiple copies, we offer discount retail pricing as follows:

Regular Retail Price: $9.95 per book
12 to 24 copies: $8.95 per book
25 or more copies: $7.95 per book

Please add $1.50 shipping for the first book, and .50 per additional book, or $6.00 additional shipping for every 12 books per order.

If you are a bookseller, retailer or hold a retail license, call us at 1-800-451-7019 or 813-951-6567 to discuss our wholesale pricing.

Look for our easy-to-use order form on the next page.

THE VETERAN'S FRIEND GROUP

Order copies of the book,
"In Your Service"

QUANTITY   @ PRICE   TOTAL

_____   _____   _____

SUBTOTAL   _____

SHIPPING   _____

TOTAL   _____

Make checks or money orders payable to:

Brann Publishing

and submit to:
Brann Publishing
26345 Dayflower Blvd.
Wesley Chapel, FL 33543

(Please note: All profits will be re-directed to helping veterans obtain the Aid & Attendance benefit.)

FOR MORE INFORMATION

Interested in learning more about The Galen Maddy Group, our financial and estate planning services, or signing up for a planning meeting to discuss our *pro bono* work of helping you or a loved one secure the Aid & Attendance Benefit? Please copy the brief information questionnaire below, fill out and mail to us at the address on the back side of this page. We'll get right back to you.

NAME:

ADDRESS:

CITY, STATE:

ZIP:

PHONE:

FAX:

E-MAIL:

VETERAN STATUS
(Years Served, Military Branch):

INTERESTED IN MORE INFORMATION?

INTERESTED IN ATTENDING A SEMINAR?

INTERESTED IN A PLANNING MEETING?

Mail to:

The Galen Maddy Group
2897 Brentwood Court
Carlsbad, CA 92008
1-800-451-7019
gmaddy@adelphia.net
www.VeteransFriend.com

ACKNOWLEDGMENTS

I would like to thank my colleagues with The Veteran's Friend Group, Merwyn J. Miller and Len Accardi, for sharing my commitment to wartime veterans by providing this *pro bono* service. An added thanks to Merwyn Miller (son of a World War II Veteran) for putting together the Qvap Trust and writing about it in Chapter 6.

Additional thanks go to my administrative assistant, Kate Seelye, to Robert Yehling of Word Journeys, Inc. (whose father, a Marine officer, served in the Korean and Vietnam wars), and to Bo Savino of Oculus Media, LLC, (whose son is a young Marine recruit), my three right hands in compiling this book. Much gratitude goes to others helping wartime veterans to obtain the benefit. This includes Galen Jones, Stephen Stone and Debra Bell, who offered several experiences to this book; Carl Anderson, for his friendship and commitment to veterans through his military service and clinical work at Veterans Village; to Tom Pizer, for his hard work in this area. Also many thanks to Tom Boyle, who attended one of my workshops and spread the word about the Aid & Attendance Benefit to everyone he knew with one of the most inspiring testimonials I've read.

The dream and commitment of producing this book would not have been a reality without the help of my dear friend Steve Scholfield. *North County Times* columnist Tom Morrow provided much-appreciated coverage of the Veteran's Friend workshops and explained the benefit to his readers.

Most of all, I thank you, fellow military veterans and/or surviving spouses of this country, for serving with the distinction and honor my colleagues and I hope to reflect in our service back to you.

ABOUT THE AUTHOR

In 2008, *In Your Service* author and U.S. Marine Corps Veteran Galen Maddy, C.F.C., CEPS, will celebrate 40 years of serving clients nationwide as founder and president of the Galen Maddy Group.

The graduate of Michigan State University is nationally recognized for his expertise and accomplishments in tax planning, financial advising and retirement planning for seniors. Board Certified as a tax consultant and former member of the Board of Directors of First Pension Savings and First Liberty Financial, Galen's commitment is to provide highest-quality service and value for senior clients and their financial planning needs.

Galen has served thousands of clients over the years, and touched the lives of many thousands more through his column, "Financial Ink," and the many workshops and guest speeches he has conducted.

In recent years, Galen has added to his already decorated portfolio by taking on the task of helping wartime veterans receive the little-known Aid and Attendance Benefit. The *pro bono* work has enabled him to touch on an aspect of his own personal history—serving during the Vietnam War—while helping to provide greater financial security for many.

Galen resides in North San Diego County, Calif., his home for many years.

Printed in the United States
96685LV00002B/289-999/A